BROCCOLI

Christopher Trotter

Photography by Caroline Trotter

© Christopher Trotter 2019

Published by Christopher Trotter.

A CIP catalogue record for this book is available from the British Library.
ISBN 978-0-9926830-7-8

Produced by Print & Design, University of St Andrews
Website: www.st-andrews.ac.uk/printanddesign

Printed by J Thomson Colour Printers

Distributed by Christopher Trotter
Tel: 07739049639

CONTENTS

INTRODUCTION

This is the seventh book in my series of little vegetable cook books and it has been such a pleasure over the years to work on the recipes and bring each book to fruition. The research, tasting, taking photos, editing and finally holding the actual book in my hands, always remains a thrill! Then because they are self-published, I also have to distribute them and this sometimes involves simply dropping them off at Waterstone's or a local farm shop and then I have a few loyal outlets further afield.

They also sell through my website www.christophertrotter.co.uk. I enjoy getting out and about to different autumn and winter fairs to sell them and talk to people who have enjoyed them. The idea behind each one is for a vegetable which is widely grown in the UK both commercially and in private gardens. So, you can really enjoy the full variety of ideas throughout the season that the vegetable is available.

COOKING PHILOSOPHY

People often ask me what style of cooking I do or what sort of food do I cook. My answer is usually "Seasonal Scottish" and then I feel that I have to qualify that. By saying that, as with all great cultures, we are an outward-looking nation and have over the centuries absorbed ideas and ingredients from all over the world. So, whilst my training was fundamentally in the grand French tradition (Larousse Gastronomique and Escoffier), over the years I have incorporated spices, "exotic" fruits and vegetables. I use fermented and pickled foods as well as foraged ingredients. But what will always remain the same is that the main ingredients, be they meat, fish or vegetable, will always be sourced from Scotland.

NOMENCLATURE AND SEASONS

The word "broccoli" covers a large variety of vegetables. In some areas of the UK it's a late winter cauliflower. To gardeners and cooks it's a short version for purple sprouting broccoli. To most people it simply means the large-headed green calabrese which is originally from Calabria in southern Italy, and because of its uniformity, the one most suited to selling through supermarkets. In this book, I have used a variety, and the specific type is only mentioned in a recipe because that is one used in the picture! But please feel free to interchange as they become available in season.

CALABRESE
It's a mild-flavoured brassica and thus is popular with children. The UK season is between June and November; outwith this period, it will have been imported. Always check the label.

PURPLE SPROUTING BROCCOLI
Probably my favourite; not often found in supermarkets because of its habit of growing in a non-uniform manner! I think it can be a close-run thing in flavour with asparagus, and simply boiled quickly or grilled, it is stunning with an hollandaise sauce. Being available in the UK from January to May, it has a much longer season and is considerably cheaper than asparagus.

TENDERSTEM
This is a hybrid of Chinese kale and purple sprouting and is a branded, trademarked name. In order for it to be available year round, a lot is imported, so I tend not to buy unless it comes from UK producers. The flavour is good, but not as good as purple sprouting.

ROMANESCO
This is a cross between cauliflower and calabrese and can be used in most of my recipes, but I have included it in my cauliflower book!

NUTRITION

Whilst broccoli is 90% water, it is also a source of vitamin K and C. Vitamin C is a powerful antioxidant and helps protect the body from free radicals. The stem also has fibre which aids digestion and helps protect against bowel cancer. It has folic acid which is good for pregnant mothers. It is also high in iron and potassium.

BROCCOLI RECIPES

BLANCHING

I use this method all through the book and it is useful when cooking in quantities for larger groups or to have cold broccoli in a salad. There are several steps that are incorporated.

PREPARATION

You need to cut your broccoli into similar-sized pieces so that they all cook at the same time. This might mean removing large stalks or cutting a criss-cross in the base to allow the stalk to cook as quickly as possible.

COOKING

Take a large pan of boiling salted water, and have ready a bowl of ice-cold water. Plunge the prepared vegetables into the boiling water; not too much at a time. You want the water to return to the boil very quickly. This may be enough cooking time for smaller, thin stems, for purple sprouting or tenderstem. Otherwise, cook for a few minutes and check for "doneness" by plunging one piece into the cold water briefly and eating it. You want a little bite or crunch. When done, lift the vegetables out with a slotted spoon and plunge into the ice-cold water.

REFRESHING

Leave them there until completely cold; this is very important as if they are still warm in the middle, they will go on cooking. The cold arrests the cooking process and keeps the gorgeous green colour. Once cool, drain thoroughly in a colander. The vegetables will keep, covered with a damp cloth in the fridge, for a few days.

REHEATING

To reheat, simply plunge in a pan of boiling water until hot through, shake off excess water, and serve. Broccoli cooked like this will keep warm, without losing colour, for some time. Or you can toss in oil or melted butter with seasonings etc. as per recipes.

PASTA WITH PURPLE SPROUTING BROCCOLI

A very simple dish which you can build on by adding other ingredients, but the colour with the flecks of red and grated cheese looks great. I use my local cheese, made by Jane Stewart.

INGREDIENTS

8 heads purple sprouting broccoli
4 tblsp cold-pressed rapeseed oil
1 red chilli, finely chopped
2 cloves garlic, peeled and finely sliced
300g pasta, penne or fusilli
Sea Salt and black pepper

Serve with grated Anster cheese and cold-pressed rape seed oil

METHOD

1 Half fill a large pan with water, bring to the boil and add salt and a splash of oil.
2 Throw the pasta into the water and cook as per pack instructions.
3 Five minutes before the pasta is cooked, add the broccoli.
4 In a frying pan, warm the chilli with the garlic in the oil.
5 When all is cooked, drain the pasta and broccoli, keeping a little cooking water, and mix with the chilli and garlic oil mixture; check for salt and add black pepper.
6 Sprinkle the grated Anster over the pasta with an extra splash of oil.

WILD PIE

Purple sprouting broccoli with wild greens pie.

A delicious, fresh, crunchy-topped pie. You can vary the greens with wild garlic or ground elder.

INGREDIENTS

2 tblsp extra virgin olive oil
Small leek, roughly chopped
Bunch spring onions or wild garlic, roughly chopped
200g nettles, washed and chopped
200g purple sprouting broccoli, blanched.
200g kale, shredded
Bunch chervil or parsley, chopped
Small bunch fennel leaves, chopped
100ml double cream
250g pack filo pastry
100g melted butter

Cheese sauce
25g butter and flour
250ml milk
30g grated cheese

METHOD

1 Preheat the oven to 180C, gas mark 4.
2 Heat the oil in a wide pan and sweat the leek and spring onions.
3 Add the nettles and kale and cook until soft; stir in the blanched broccoli and the herbs.
4 Make a cheese sauce.
5 Mix with the greens, and stir in the cream.
6 Lay 3 layers of filo in a 35 × 40 cm dish, brushing each sheet with melted butter.
7 Add the greens mixture.
8 Cover with the remaining filo, brushing each sheet with butter.
9 Bake in the oven until crisp and lightly browned, about 20 minutes.

BROCCOLI SALAD WITH FRESH CRAB AND GRAPEFRUIT

Living in the East Neuk of Fife means I have access to fantastic sea food and Crail has a great reputation for its crab. This fresh-tasting salad is perfect on a summer's evening.

INGREDIENTS

400g broccoli, blanched and refreshed.
100g lamb's lettuce
1 cucumber, peeled and cut in chunks
1 avocado, peeled and sliced
2 pink grapefruit, segmented (keep the juice)
200g white crab meat
Coarse sea salt
1 tblsp extra virgin olive oil
Freshly ground black pepper

Dressing
1 red chilli, seeded and chopped
Zest and juice of a lemon
Grapefruit juice

METHOD

1 Make the dressing, using enough grapefruit juice to make a clean, fresh flavour.
2 Dress a salad bowl with the broccoli broken into small florets and scatter a little dressing over.
3 Build up the salad as you wish with the cucumber and lamb's lettuce. Dot the crab here and there with the grapefruit segments and then the avocado.
4 Finish with the remaining dressing and some chopped, fresh herbs and a sprinkle of coarse sea salt.

PSB AND SALSIFY
WITH CAPER BUTTER

Whilst I am all for seasonal cooking, I also like to promote unusual vegetables which historically have been grown in this country, and salsify is one such. Ask your farm shop to grow it!

INGREDIENTS

2 lemons cut in half, juice one and set the juice aside
4 salsify roots
400g purple sprouting broccoli, trimmed weight
100g cold butter

2 tblsp small capers
2 tblsp chopped chives
2 tblsp flat leaf parsley
2 tblsp chopped tarragon
2 tblsp chopped dill
Salt and pepper

METHOD

1 Bring a pan of water to the boil, add salt and the remaining lemon halves, squeezing the juice out as you do.
2 Peel the salsify and cut into 3 batons, put straight into the boiling water and cook until al dente, about 10 minutes; drain and allow to dry.
3 Cook the broccoli in the same water, drain and set aside in a large bowl.
4 Cut the cooked salsify batons into quarters lengthwise.
4 Heat half the butter and, as it foams, add the salsify and cook quickly until golden brown, pour onto the broccoli, mix together and season. You can either leave them in the bowl or dress them in a clean warm one.
6 Return the pan to the heat and add the remaining butter, allow it to go nut brown and then away from the heat add the remaining lemon juice, capers and herbs, season and sprinkle over the prepared vegetables.

Note: don't worry if you don't have all of the herbs just use what you have!

BROCCOLI, CAULIFLOWER AND ANSTER CHEESE WALNUT CRUMBLE

Making use again of my local cheese. It's a crumbly Cheshire-style cheese. The walnuts add a sweetness and crunch.

INGREDIENTS

1 medium cauliflower cut in large florets
1 head of broccoli, cut into florets
2 cloves garlic, crushed with salt
3 tblsp extra virgin olive oil
Salt and pepper
50g walnuts, roughly chopped
50g butter
50g rolled oats
40g breadcrumbs
150ml double cream
125g Anster cheese, grated

METHOD

1 Preheat the oven to 220C, gas mark 7.
2 Mix the prepared vegetables and garlic with the oil and seasoning and roast in a tin for 15 minutes.
3 Rub the butter into the oats and then add the breadcrumbs and broken nuts to form a rough crumble; season.
4 When the vegetables have cooked for 15 minutes, mix through the cream and grated cheese. Sprinkle the crumble over the top and return to the oven for 20 minutes or until crisp and brown.

SALMON WITH BROCCOLI, LIME, GINGER AND CHILLI

A colourful, simple, one dish recipe.

INGREDIENTS

400g broccoli, broken in to florets
2 tblsp sesame oil
2 cloves garlic, crushed with salt
1 shallot, peeled and finely chopped
Chunk of ginger grated, about 2cm
2 tblsp nam pla sauce
4 salmon fillets @ 180g each
3 tblsp cold-pressed rapeseed oil
Zest and juice of 2 limes
Bunch coriander, roughly chopped
2 tsp sunflower seeds, toasted

METHOD

1 Preheat the oven to 180C, gas mark 6.
2 Mix the sesame oil with the garlic, shallot, ginger and nam pla. Combine with the broccoli, put in a roasting tin and place the salmon fillets on top. Cover in tin foil and bake for 20 minutes.
3 Make a dressing with the rapeseed oil, lime zest and juice and coriander, check for seasoning.
4 When the salmon is cooked, sprinkle over the dressing and leave for a few minutes before serving with the toasted sunflower seeds.

CHARGRILLED BROCCOLI WITH CHILLI AND GARLIC

A useful addition to the barbeque; the dressing can be prepared in advance and heated through on the bbq.

INGREDIENTS

2 heads of broccoli, broken into florets
6 tblsp olive oil
4 cloves garlic, thinly sliced
2 red chillies, thinly sliced
1 tblsp toasted, flaked almonds

METHOD

1 Blanche and refresh the broccoli.
2 Once the broccoli has been refreshed, dab dry on kitchen paper to remove as much moisture as possible. Toss in 3 tblsp of the oil. Use a barbeque or a ribbed griddle pan at a high heat, place the florets on the heat, giving each piece space so as not to reduce the heat. Cook just long enough to get char marks, then turn them over and repeat. Transfer to a bowl.
3 Place the remaining oil in a sauce pan and cook the garlic and chilli, to lightly colour. Pour over the broccoli and serve with a sprinkling of toasted flaked almonds.

PSB WITH PHEASANT, RICE AND LIME

A simple take on an Indonesian dish. Recently, I have taken on the role of managing the food hall and theatre at the Scottish Game Fair and I am trying to encourage people to eat more pheasant.

INGREDIENTS

2 tblsp arachide oil
1 onion, peeled and sliced
1 red pepper cut in half, seeded and sliced
4 pheasant breasts, cut in strips
200g purple broccoli, halved lengthwise
3 cloves garlic, peeled and chopped
500g cooked rice
4 spring onions, sliced diagonally

4 eggs
4 tblsp soy sauce
1 tsp light brown sugar
Juice of a lime

Garnish
¼ cucumber sliced into matchsticks
2 tsp unsalted cashews
1 tblsp chopped coriander leaves

METHOD

1 Heat a frying pan with 1 tblsp oil and fry the onion until soft and golden brown; remove and set aside.
2 Add a little more oil and cook the red pepper and pheasant for a few minutes, then add the garlic, spring onions and broccoli. Cook, turning the pheasant strips occasionally for a few minutes. Stir in the rice gently, so as not to crush it; you are just reheating it.
3 In a separate pan, heat the remaining oil, beat the eggs in a bowl and pour into the pan; cook as for an omelette, until just firm all over. Tip onto a board and slice into ribbons and mix with the rice, soy, sugar, seasoning and onions.
4 Heat through adding the lime juice. Serve with the nuts, cucumber and coriander sprinkled over the top.

BROCCOLI IN A CRISP BATTER WITH TOMATO SALSA

This makes a lovely sharing first course or to have with drinks. You can use purple broccoli for this as well. I have used my local cheese but a strong cheddar-style cheese is fine.

INGREDIENTS

Salsa
1 red pepper
4 ripe tomatoes, blanched, skinned, seeded and diced
2 tblsp olive oil
1 clove garlic, peeled and crushed with salt
1 red chilli, deseeded and finely chopped
1tblsp basil leaves, shredded

Salt and black pepper
Broccoli and batter
1 egg
100ml double cream
40g aged Anster, grated
400g purple or tenderstem broccoli, trimmed, blanched and refreshed.
Plain flour
Vegetable oil

METHOD

1 Roast the pepper until blackened all over, pop into a plastic bag until cool and slip off the skin, remove the seeds and dice the flesh.
2 Mix with the diced tomatoes, chilli, garlic and basil, add olive oil to get a dipping texture and season.
3 Half fill a large pan with vegetable oil, and heat to about 175C.
4 Create a batter from the beaten egg, cream and grated cheese, season.
5 Toss the broccoli in the flour, shaking off excess and dip into the batter, drop into the oil and fry for two minutes until lightly browned. Cook in batches so that the oil keeps its temperature.

BROCCOLI WITH BEETROOT AND TOASTED SEEDS, SERVED WARM

A colourful vegetable side dish, or good with a barbecue. I prefer to roast my own beetroot (See my Beetroot book) but you can buy it ready cooked.

INGREDIENTS

4 heads broccoli, cut in florets, blanched and refreshed.
250g beetroot.
2 tblsp cold-pressed rapeseed oil
3 tblsp mixed seeds, sunflower, sesame, fennel
1tblsp soy sauce
1 tblsp finely chopped chives
Juice of a lemon
Salt and pepper

METHOD

1 Heat the oven to 200C, gas mark 6, place the beetroot in a roasting tin, sprinkle with oil and put in oven for about 45 minutes, until just cooked. Slip off the skins, cut in wedges and keep warm.
2 Take a large frying pan and add 1 tblsp rapeseed oil and gently fry the seeds, to colour lightly.
3 Add the broccoli and stir to heat through, followed by the soy and then the beetroot and when warm dress in a suitable dish.
4 Mix the remaining oil with the lemon juice, season and sprinkle over followed by the chives.

BROCCOLI, EGG AND NEW POTATOES WITH TUNA DIP

I love Ayrshire potatoes, and it is worth the wait as the season progresses; avoiding tasteless Jersey Royals, enjoying a few Cornish epicures and then falling hungrily on lovely, waxy, earthy Ayrshires. It's a seasonal marker for me.

INGREDIENTS

500g broccoli or purple, blanched and refreshed.
500g new Ayrshire potatoes
4 eggs, soft boiled and cooled
2 heads chicory (Belgian endive)

Dip
Tin tuna 160g
1 tsp wholegrain mustard
1 tsp smooth mustard
2 tblsp mayo
2 tblsp yoghourt
Juice of half a lemon
Cayenne pepper to sprinkle
Salt and pepper

METHOD

1 Wash the Ayrshires under a tap, rubbing off any mud or loose skin, but do not peel. Place in a pan of salted water and bring to the boil; simmer until just cooked. Drain and allow to cool. Cut in half.
2 Make the dip by mixing the tuna and mustards together until smooth, then fold in the mayo and yoghourt, season with lemon juice and salt and pepper. Place in a suitable bowl and sprinkle over the cayenne.
3 Place the bowl in the centre of a large dish or plate. Arrange the broccoli florets and leaves from the chicory around with the halved potatoes, and the eggs cut into quarters.

BROCCOLI SALAD WITH AN EASTERN DRESSING

A simple but delicious warm side dish

1 Head of broccoli, cut into florets
1 clove of garlic, peeled
Small lump of fresh ginger, grated
Pinch sugar
1 tblsp cider vinegar
2 tsp soy sauce
1 tblsp toasted sesame oil
2 tsp toasted sesame seeds
1 shallot, finely chopped
Salt and pepper

METHOD

1 Blanche and refresh the broccoli; drain and keep warm.
2 Make a dressing by crushing the garlic, ginger and sugar in a mortar and then add the oil, vinegar and soy.
3 Toss the cooked broccoli in the dressing and allow to cool a little; check for seasoning.
4 Dress in a suitable bowl with the sesame seeds and chopped shallot.

The photo shows raw ruby chard stalks also sprinkled over the top. Beetroot stalks are good as well.

BROCCOLI SLAW

I never liked the word "slaw" as its sounds slovenly, being the shortened version of coleslaw, but then I realised that actually slaw simply means salad and the Dutch Koolsla means cabbage salad. So, suddenly, "slovenly slaw" is back in my dictionary!

INGREDIENTS

3 carrots peeled and cut into matchsticks
1 red onion, peeled and sliced thinly
2 heads broccoli, sliced
2 red apples, cored and sliced into matchsticks
Juice of a lemon
200ml plain yoghourt
1 tsp fennel seeds

METHOD

1 Mix all the vegetables and apples together.
2 Make a dressing with the lemon and yoghourt.
3 Mix together and dress with fennel seeds.

BROCCOLI RICE

This idea was taken from an Indian recipe for lobster and you can mix lobster meat through it if you like! It's quite fun as a change and you get your greens and carbs all in one.

INGREDIENTS

½ head of broccoli
2 tblsp sunflower oil
40g butter
1 tblsp mustard seeds
Chunk of fresh ginger (2cm), peeled and chopped
Clove of garlic, peeled and chopped
2 green chillies, chopped
1 tsp curry leaves (optional)
2 shallots, peeled and sliced
160g basmati rice
400ml vegetable stock
2 tblps chopped coriander

METHOD

1 Place the broccoli in boiling salted water until just cooked. Drain and shake dry. Whizz to puree in a food processor and set aside.
2 Heat the oil and butter in a frying pan and add the mustard seeds, as they start to spit, stir in the shallots, ginger, garlic, chillies and curry leaves. Cook gently, stirring occasionally for a few minutes.
3 Stir in the rice, and sauté together for 2 minutes. Pour in the stock and simmer until the liquid is almost absorbed. Stir in the broccoli puree and cook until the rice is done.
4 Serve with the coriander sprinkled over.

PURPLE SPROUTING BROCCOLI WITH ANCHOVIES AND OLIVE OIL

Rowley Leigh has to take credit for this idea (although he credits Simon Hopkinson). It makes a delicious first course.

8 salted anchovy fillets
Juice of a lemon
50ml extra virgin olive oil
1 tsp crushed black pepper
750g purple sprouting broccoli

1 Chop the anchovy fillets and then pound them in a mortar with the lemon juice, olive oil and black pepper.
2 Place the broccoli in boiling, salted water until just cooked, drain through a colander and shake to remove excess water.
3 Toss in the anchovy dressing, serve immediately.

PURPLE SPROUTING BROCCOLI WITH BUTTER AND ANSTER CHEESE

I never miss an opportunity to promote my local cheese; the only one produced in Fife and made by the wonderful Jane Stewart. This also shows another way of cooking broccoli without boiling. But it is important that the pieces are all the same size.

INGREDIENTS

400g broccoli
2 tsp butter
Salt and pepper
Boiling water
100g Anster cheese

METHOD

1 Heat a large pan with lid and add the butter. When it melts and starts to foam up, throw in the broccoli and mix it round, coating thoroughly with the butter.
2 Add a little salt and a few grounds of pepper, then pour in enough boiling water to just cover the base of the pan and quickly cover with the lid.
3 When the water has all gone, remove the lid and toss around to clear any excess water. Serve in a suitable bowl with the cheese scattered in thin slivers.

SAVOY BROCCOLI AND POTATO TART

Based on Tartiflette, the Savoyard cheese tart using Reblochon, but a soft brie or camembert will do instead.

INGREDIENTS

800g potatoes, cut into small cubes
1 tblsp extra virgin olive oil
Large onion, peeled and chopped
200g smoked, streaky bacon cut in lardons
500g broccoli, cut in small florets
150ml dry white wine
400g Reblochon, cut into cubes like the potato
3 tblsp crème fraiche
Salt and pepper

METHOD

1 Heat the oven to 200C, gas mark 6.
2 Cook the potatoes for 10 minutes in water, drain and set aside.
3 Blanche and refresh the broccoli.
4 Heat a large frying pan with the oil and fry the onion and lardons until cooked but not crisp.
5 Add the wine and simmer gently for 5 minutes, remove from the heat.
6 Stir in the potatoes, cubes of cheese, crème fraiche and season.
7 Take an ovenproof serving dish and pour in half the potato mixture, scatter over the broccoli and then finish with the remaining potato mixture.
8 Bake in the oven for 30 minutes until lightly brown and bubbling.

BROCCOLI WITH WET GARLIC

Wet or green garlic is the young fresh garlic, before is has been dried and hardened for storing. You can eat it whole, as the separating "skins" are tender and easy to eat. This also shows you how to use broccoli stalks.

INGREDIENTS

500g broccoli
3 tblsp olive oil
1 head wet or green garlic, chopped
1 tsp caster sugar
Handful chopped wild garlic, if available
150ml white wine
1 tsp chopped marjoram
Zest of half a lemon

METHOD

1 Cut the broccoli into small florets; peel the stem and cut into a small dice.
2 Heat the oil in a large heavy-based pan; throw in the diced stalks and wet garlic and cook for a few minutes. Add the florets, sugar, wild garlic and wine. Bring to the boil.
3 Add the marjoram and lemon zest and cook until broccoli is tender; season and serve.

BROCCOLI IN RED WINE

An unusual dish, ideal as a first course or a vegetarian main.

INGREDIENTS

500g Broccoli
1 onion, peeled and sliced thinly
50g black olives pitted and halved
4 anchovy fillets chopped
50g Anster cheese
4 tblsp olive oil
175ml red wine

METHOD

1 Turn the oven to 180C, gas mark 4.
2 Cut the broccoli into small florets and peel the stalk and cut into small batons;
   blanche and refresh the florets.
3 Place the other ingredients in an oven dish in layers, onion first then the broccoli stalks, olives, anchovies, cheese and wine; drizzle with oil. Cover with foil and bake for 45 minutes.
4 Remove the foil, turn the oven up to 200C, gas mark 6 and place the blanched, refreshed broccoli on top. Sprinkle with the cheese and oil and bake for another 15 minutes.

DEEP FRIED BROCCOLI INDIAN STYLE

A spicy batter which can be used for lots of vegetables but especially good for broccoli and cauliflower.

4 tblsp gram flour
1 tblsp rice flour
Pinch chilli powder
1 tsp ground coriander
100ml sparkling mineral water
Broccoli florets
Vegetable oil

METHOD

1 Mix the flours together, adding the chilli and coriander.
Stir in the water until you get quite a thick batter; it should coat the vegetable but not too thickly.
2 Half fill a large pan with vegetable oil, heat to about 175C and carefully dip the florets in the batter; allow to drip off a little, then plunge into the hot oil.
3 When brown and crisp, drain on kitchen paper and serve with suitable dips.

BROCCOLI, BEAN AND PASTA SOUP

An Italian-style soup, full of flavours and really a meal in itself. You can play around with different herbs and it works with different beans as well. The picture shows little rounds of toast with the cheese melted on top.

INGREDIENTS

2 tblsp olive oil
1 onion peeled and chopped
5 cloves garlic, crushed
1 tsp fresh oregano or marjoram, chopped
Sprig of thyme
400g broccoli, stalks finely chopped and the florets broken into small pieces

400g can of haricot beans
800ml chicken stock or 'Marigold'
100g small pasta shells
2 tblsp grated parmesan, (unusual for me, I know, but it is an Italian-style soup!)
Sea salt and freshly-ground black pepper

METHOD

1 Heat the olive oil in a large pan, and sweat the onion gently for a few minutes to soften.
2 Stir in the garlic, herbs and broccoli stalks, and cook for a few minutes,
3 Tip in the beans and stock and allow to simmer for 10 minutes
4 Add the pasta and florets and cook until the pasta has reached al dente. Season.
5 Serve sprinkled liberally with parmesan.

WARM SALAD OF BROCCOLI, WITH LEEKS AND CANNELLINI

A "modern" salad with the leeks attractively marked with a griddle; if you can't be bothered to do that, don't! But still use blanched leeks; the dressing really brings out the earthiness of the leek. And, of course, my local cheese!

INGREDIENTS

4 leeks, trimmed and cut in half lengthwise
2 heads broccoli, broken into florets
400g tin of cannellini beans, drained
1 tblsp chopped parsley
2 tblsp balsamic vinegar
2 tblsp olive oil
1 tblsp Anster cheese, grated
Sea salt and freshly-ground black pepper

METHOD

1 Blanche the leeks in boiling salted water for 2 minutes, drain and dry well. Keep the water.
2 Heat a griddle pan, brush lightly with a little oil and press the leeks firmly on to it. Colour with ridges on both sides; allow to cool a little and cut into strips across the grain.
3 Cook the broccoli florets in the saved leek water, until just cooked, and drain well.
4 Make a dressing with the oil and vinegar, add the parsley, broccoli and beans. Dress gently with the leeks and serve with grated cheese.

ROAST BROCCOLI WITH CHILLI AND SOY

I think the deep green colour of broccoli flecked with red chilli is just beautiful. This roasted version avoids water, and the stalks cooked together with the florets give a crunch. Very good as a first course or a side dish.

INGREDIENTS

2 heads broccoli, broken into florets and the stalks into batons
2 tblsp olive oil
2 cloves garlic, thinly sliced
1 red chilli, thinly sliced
2 tblsp soy sauce
Juice of a lemon
2 tsp toasted sesame seeds

METHOD

1 Turn the oven to 200C, gas mark 6.
2 Toss the broccoli in the oil and spread out in a roasting tin and cook for 10 minutes.
3 Add the garlic and chilli, mix through, and return to the oven for another 5 minutes.
4 Stir in the soy and lemon juice. Serve sprinkled with the toasted sesame seeds.

PURPLE SPROUTING BROCCOLI CAESAR SALAD

I am a great fan of the Dean and Deluca school of recipes in which they provide the classic (as they see it!) recipe and then variations. It reminds me of my time in the Savoy in London, where the diktat was: "There are three ways of doing things, the right way, the wrong way and the Savoy way". Here is my variation on the D and D way. This also works with calabrese, but cut the stalks into thin strips and cook as per the psb until just crunchy.

INGREDIENTS

500g purple sprouting broccoli, trimmed, blanched and refreshed.
6 anchovy fillets
4 cloves garlic
1 egg, boiled for 30 seconds
1 tsp Dijon mustard

4 tsp lemon juice
175ml virgin olive oil
4 slices white bread (sourdough is perfect), cut into small cubes
Parmesan curls

METHOD

1 Crush two cloves of garlic with the anchovies to create a paste.
2 Drop the egg into a bowl with the anchovy paste. Whisk in the mustard and lemon juice then, in a steady stream, pour on 125ml of the oil to form a light mayonnaise.
3 Turn the oven to 180C, gas mark 6 and heat the remainder of the oil in an oven-proof dish with two cloves of garlic and allow to infuse for 10 minutes. Discard the garlic, toss the bread cubes in the oil and bake in the oven for 10 minutes until golden brown – croutons.
4 Coat the broccoli in the dressing and place in a bowl; sprinkle over the croutons and finish with the parmesan.

BROCCOLI AND DUNSYRE BLUE CHEESE SOUP

A favourite of my son Byam, it is equally good chilled as it is hot. I used to add double cream but found that with the quality of the Dunsyre blue cheese, it was not necessary. The creamy texture came from the cheese.

INGREDIENTS

1 onion, peeled and sliced
25g butter
350g broccoli, stalks sliced separate from the florets
400ml stock, boiling
75g Dunsyre (or other) blue cheese
Sea salt and freshly-ground black pepper
Grated nutmeg
1 tblsp toasted, flaked almonds

METHOD

1 In a large pan, soften the onion in the butter over a low heat for 5 minutes.
2 Add the sliced broccoli stalks and stir to coat on the buttery, oniony mixture.
3 Pour in the stock and bring to a gentle simmer. Cook for 10 minutes.
4 Add the florets and simmer until they are cooked. Away from the heat, add the cheese and stir to melt, then liquidise until smooth.
5 Reheat if necessary and season with salt and pepper and a little grated nutmeg.
6 Serve with the flaked almonds, sprinkled over.

RAW BROCCOLI SALAD WITH LARDONS AND MAYONNAISE

The idea for this delicious salad came from my wife Caroline; the broccoli is raw and so has to be broken into small pieces.

INGREDIENTS

The florets from 2 heads of broccoli, use the stalks elsewhere
100g bacon lardons
1 shallot, peeled and finely chopped
2 tblsp mayonnaise
1 tsp Dijon mustard
Juice of half a lemon

METHOD

1 Break the florets into very small pieces and place in a serving dish.
2 Heat a frying pan and fry the lardons until almost crisp. Away from the heat, throw in the shallot and mix to just soften. Tip onto the broccoli and mix through.
3 Mix the mayonnaise, mustard and lemon juice to create a coating texture and dress the broccoli.

CHICKEN AND BROCCOLI NOODLE SOUP

The Americans swear by the health-giving qualities of "chickensoup", so imagine how good it is with broccoli!

INGREDIENTS

1 whole chicken
2 bay leaves
1 tsp peppercorns
6 tblsp fish sauce
140g tin bamboo shoots
280g dry rice noodles
280g purple sprouting broccoli

Juice of a lime
2 spring onions, thickly sliced
1 tblsp chopped coriander
2 shallots, peeled and sliced
3 red chillies, thinly sliced
Sea salt and freshly-ground black pepper

METHOD

1 Place the chicken in a large pan, into which it will fit snugly, cover with water and add the bay leaves and peppercorns. Bring to the boil then lower heat and simmer for an hour until cooked. Allow to cool.
2 When cool, strain the stock into another pan and strip the meat off the carcass. Discard the bones, pepper corns and bay leaves.
3 Bring the stock to the boil, season with salt and fish sauce.
4 Blanche and refresh the broccoli, using the stock as your water.
5 Add the bamboo shoots and noodles to the stock and cook for a few minutes.
6 Break the chicken into spoon-size chunks and return to the pot; add the broccoli and reheat. Add the lime juice.
7 Serve in individual bowls with the spring onions, chilli and coriander as a garnish.

PURPLE SPROUTING BROCCOLI SALAD WITH PANEER AND CUMIN APPLE RAITA

I make paneer when I have a large amount of milk going off! There are easy on-line recipes. You can use any sort of mild cheese for this if paneer is not available.

INGREDIENTS

250g broccoli blanched and refreshed.
2 tblsp vegetable oil
1 tsp mustard seeds
225g paneer cheese diced
Juice of a lemon
2 large carrots peeled and grated
2 tsp ground cumin
2 tsp ground coriander
1 tsp chilli powder

Raita
1 red, sharp apple (Cox or Braeburn), grated
100g natural yoghurt
2 tsp cumin seeds, crushed
1 tsp sea salt

METHOD

1 In a wide frying pan or wok, fry the mustard seeds in oil until they pop; add the diced paneer and allow to colour at the edges, stir in the lemon juice.
2 Stir in the spices and the grated carrot. Finally, add the broccoli and heat through.
3 Make the raita by mixing the ingredients together and lightly season with salt. Either serve with the raita scattered over or allow guests to help themselves to both.

BROCCOLI A LA GRECQUE

This is an idea from the distant days of the hors d'oeuvres trolley, at the Savoy, which I used to help create. It is interesting how that term has gone out of use but we now have "small plates". Plus ca change! I am indebted to my friend Jacques Eza, former Savoy head chef, for help with this.

INGREDIENTS

250g broccoli florets blanched and refreshed.
4 tblsp water
4 tblsp olive oil
4 tblsp lemon juice
2 tsp coriander seeds
3 shallots, peeled and sliced
1 tsp pepper corns
2 or 3 parsley stalks

METHOD

1 Put all the ingredients, except the broccoli, into a pan and bring to a boil; simmer for 5 minutes.
2 Place the prepared broccoli in a suitable dish and pour the hot liquid over it, making sure the broccoli is covered. Leave to cool.
3 Once cool, refrigerate and it will keep for a few days. Serve with cold meats or other "small plates".

BIOGRAPHIES

CAROLINE TROTTER is a freelance photographer and works across a wide variety of subjects. Weddings are her main area of work but she also does portraits, both human and animal – horses, dogs etc. Caroline covers events for associations such as Fife Chamber of Commerce and provides business portraits for websites and marketing purposes, and food photography for websites and restaurants. She also runs photography courses from home. She is a qualified member of the Master Photographers Association and the Society of Wedding and Portrait photographers.

www.carolinetrotter.co.uk

CHRISTOPHER TROTTER is Fife's Food Ambassador, an honorary title bestowed on him for his work promoting food from Fife. He is also a freelance chef, cookery writer and food commentator, appearing on programmes such as BBC Radio Scotland's Kitchen Café and Kitchen Garden. He is a member of The Guild of Food Writers and is a sought-after speaker at events and after dinner. As a consultant, he has worked with agencies as diverse as Argyll and the Island's Enterprise and The National Trust for Scotland. Christopher also provides cookery classes and food tours and he is passionate about fresh produce in its season.

www.fifefoodambassador.co.uk

They have two children and two dogs and live in rural Fife.

CHRISTOPHER TROTTER

This is my sixth book in my vegetable series, so if you like this one, do look out for the others, *Beetroot*, *Courgette*, *Kale*, *Carrot* and *Cauliflower*. You can get them from my website (Christophertrotter.co.uk). I also have other cook books available, have a look on line (*The Whole Hog*, *The Whole Cow* and various on Scottish cooking and gastronomy). I have also produced a "boxed set" of all six books which make an excellent gift as you will have all of the books in a neat box so that you will never loose them!

Here are a few other things that I do which may be of interest to you:

COOKING CLASSES
These are all bespoke, based on whatever you want to do.

An ideal present for a couple or a family. I can travel! Or why not come to beautiful Fife (www.welcometofife.com) for a holiday and come to my kitchen.

A few ideas… Vegetables, shellfish, game, fish, fruit, Scottish classics, a seasonal menu…

FOOD TOURS
These can be a simple tour round Fife, which is my region in Scotland, showing you where food is grown and produced, we can visit cheesemakers, growers, farmers etc. see where the lobster and shellfish are landed and enjoy a simple meal of fresh seasonal produce. Or I can organise a larger group to do a food based tour over any part of Scotland from Galloway to Orkney and all in between!

PRIVATE CHEF
I will come to your home or holiday lodge and prepare for whatever occasion you are looking for, just get in touch. One of these jobs is to work in France providing the food for a "Lotte Birk" cooking workshop with my friend and Lotte Birk trainer Tina Roscoe.
https://www.facebook.com/LotteBerkBarreRetreats

07739049639
ct@christophertrotter.co.uk
christophertrotter.co.uk

ACKNOWLEDGEMENTS

As a member of the Guild of Food Writers, I have been inspired by past members and current ones; some of whose recipe I have used in previous books, such as Rowley Leigh, Lindsey Bareham and Sybil Kapoor. The Guild is a wonderful organisation; supporting good writing about food and encouraging young writers to embark on a writing career.

Thanks also to the East of Scotland growers who have supported this book and to the many local shops and growers in my native Fife who either sell the books or give me ideas. Bruce Bennet at Pillars of Hercules, The Pollock family at the award-winning Ardross farm shop, Loch Leven's larder, to name a few. Waterstone's book shop who encouraged me to start the series with Beetroot in 2013; the Welcome to Fife team on Fife Council, Ann, John and Karen whose support in all my activities is hugely appreciated. Last, but not least of course, is Duncan Stewart at the print and design depart of St Andrews University, who brings each project together.

NOTES

- All butter is unsalted.
- All black pepper should be freshly ground.
- Arachide oil is ground nut oi.
- Gram flour is also called chick pea flour and is a staple of north Indian diet.
- Anster cheese is the local cheese made with unpasteurised milk by the St Andrews Farmhouse Cheese Company.
- Stock – 'Marigold', this is an excellent vegetable stock available in good farm shops.

EAST OF SCOTLAND GROWERS

ESG are a farmer owned cooperative based in Cupar, in the heart of Fife, possibly Scotland's most arable region. Our main crops are Broccoli and Cauliflower along with a wider range of vegetable crops produced in the fertile Scottish soils across a 180 mile radius. As a result we are able to able to harness the variations of soil, climate to create a year round growing season for a whole variety of vegetables, including Broccoli, cauliflower onions and cabbage.

Established in 1987, with the purpose of providing the individual grower the benefits of being part of a larger group by allowing all members to grow together for the future. To this day ESG is still focused on achieving its founding aim by providing the maximum return to grower.

ESG is the largest producer of Broccoli in the UK and one of the largest in Europe with product currently going pre-pack, processing and traditional market outlets.

The East of Scotland is the best Broccoli growing area in the UK due the climate, ability to control disease and the facility to irrigate 100% of crops if required.

Broccoli is a seasonal crop and is harvested June to November, Tenderstem June to November and Purple sprouting broccoli November to May.

East of Scotland Growers